The
BERMUDA TRIANGLE

The Strange & Unexplained Mysteries of the Deep

Anna Revell

Copyright © 2017.

All rights reserved. No part of this publication may be reproduced, distributed, or transmitted in any form or by any means, including photocopying, recording, or other electronic or mechanical methods, without the prior written permission of the publisher, except in the case of brief quotations embodied in critical reviews and certain other noncommercial uses permitted by copyright law.

This book is intended for informational and entertainment purposes only. The publisher limits all liability arising from this work to the fullest extent of the law.

Table of Contents

Introduction

The Mary Celeste

The Strange Encounter of the Ellen Austin

The Disappearance of the U.S.S. Cyclops

The Mystery of the Carroll A. Deering

The Disappearance of Flight 19

The Disappearance of the Douglas DC-3

The Mystery of the Great Isaac Lighthouse

Explanations for Bermuda Triangle.

Introduction

The Bermuda Triangle is a loosely defined area of the western part of the North Atlantic Ocean where numerous aircraft and ships have reported strange occurrences, with some completely vanishing without trace. While some people dismiss the idea that there is something strange happening in the area, it is after all one of the busiest shipping lanes in the world with aircraft regularly flying over it, others remain convinced that a murky secret lurks in the waters of the Bermuda Triangle.

As early as the 15th century people were reporting strange activity in the western part of the North Atlantic Ocean. In 1492 Christopher Columbus experienced odd lights and strange compass readings. Despite this, and many other incidents and disappearances in the area over the next few centuries, it wasn't until the latter half of the twentieth century that the idea of the Bermuda Triangle was firmly established.

The writer Vincent Gaddis was one of the first people to define the boundaries of the Bermuda Triangle. In a 1964 edition of Argosy, a pulp magazine, he positioned its three points as being in Miami on the Florida peninsula, San Juan in Puerto Rico and the island of Bermuda in the mid-Atlantic.

These boundaries are not definitive, the seize of the Bermuda Triangle can vary from 500,000 square miles to 1,510,000 square miles depending on which account you are reading.

Consequently the determination of which incidents occur inside the Bermuda Triangle depends on the writer or report you are reading. This only fuels the debate regarding the authenticity of the Bermuda Triangle.

The first written suggestions of unusual disappearances in the Bermuda Triangle area appeared in an article published on the 17th of September, 1950 by Edward Van Winkle Jones in The Miami Herald. A short article a few years later in Fate magazine by George V. Sand, "Sea Mystery at Our Back Door" expanded on Jones' original idea discussing the mysterious disappearance of several planes and ships.

Over the course of the next two decades the idea of mysterious disappearances in the Bermuda Triangle took hold on the public's imagination with numerous articles, books, TV. Programs and films covering the subject. Despite being a relatively new idea investigators and writers looked back into history finding numerous mysterious disappearances and incidents which have retrospectively been attributed to the Bermuda Triangle.

Over the next few chapters we will look at some of the most famous incidents to occur in these strange waters before discussing some of the possible explanations for the Bermuda Triangle.

The Mary Celeste

Arguably the most famous ghost ship the Mary Celeste was found sailing off the coast of Portugal heading towards the Strait of Gibraltar on the 4th of December 1872. There was no crew on board and no sign of why they had abandoned ship.

Originally named "The Amazon" the Mary Celeste was built at shipyards in Spencer Island, Nova Scotia, Canada in 1861. A brigantine she was 101 foot long, almost 25 foot wide and displaced 282 tons of water.

Since she first took to the waters superstitious sailors whispered that the Mary Celeste was a bad ship. A number of incidents only served to cement this belied.

These incidents included a collision with a fishing dam which damaged her hull on her maiden voyage. When she was being repaired in the shipyards a fire broke out on board.

On her first Atlantic crossing the Mary Celeste collided with a two masted ship which sank in the straits of Dover. After again undergoing repairs she returned to America where she ran aground off Cow Bay, Nova Scotia. Of the Mary Celeste's many owners few made a profit. The majority went bankrupt.

In October 1872 the Mary Celeste was being prepared to sail from New York to Genoa, Italy. The captain of the ship was 37 year old Benjamin Briggs. Briggs' 30-year old wife

Sarah and 2-year-old child were to accompany him.

There were also seven experienced sailors on board. Captain Briggs was an experienced and able seaman who had captained five ships before taking command of the Mary Celeste. He had spent most of his life on the ocean's waves.

On the 7th of November, 1872 the Mary Celeste set sail. As well as the crew and the Briggs family, on board was a cargo of 1701 barrels of raw commercial alcohol. Valued at $35,000 the cargo was fully insured. As the Mary Celeste left port those watching on the quayside didn't realize that this was the last time that anybody would see of the crew of the Mary Celeste.

Almost a month after she sailed from New York, on the 4th of December, a British Empire vessel named Dei Gratia came within sight of the Mary Celeste as they sailed the coast of Portugal. Despite still being under sail the Dei Gratia realized that something was wrong with the Mary Celeste. After placing her under observation they realized that she was apparently abandoned.

When the crew of the Dei Gratia boarded the Mary Celeste they could find not a single soul on board. No sign of a struggle was reported nor was there any obvious reason why the crew would suddenly disappear.

While the assumed route of the Mary Celeste should have kept her north of the traditional parameters of the Bermuda Triangle many attribute her crews' mysterious disappearance to the Triangle. After all what else could explain why a seaworthy ship would be so suddenly abandoned? The weather was fine and food and water supplies were plentiful. Its crew were all able seamen and trustworthy.

Suggestions that pirates were responsible for the disappearance of the crew of the Mary Celeste can probably be dismissed. No incidents of piracy had been reported in the Straits of Gibraltar for at least a decade, probably because the area was heavily patrolled by the British Navy, further derails the piracy theory. As does the fact that the personal belongings of those on board remained untouched.

Some have suggested that the crew of the Dei Gratia, the ship that found the Mary Celeste adrift, were responsible. They suggest that the Dei Gratia had caught up with the Mary Celeste and boarded the ship under false pretenses before killing everybody on board. The crew of the Dei Gratia then fabricated the story of the ghost ship adrift off the Portuguese coast in order to claim salvage rights.

This seems unlikely- the Dei Gratia left port a week after the Mary Celeste and would have been unable to catch it. If the Dei Gratia had caught up there was no sign of a struggle on board. Also the captain of the Dei Gratia, Captain Morehouse, was a good friend of Captain Briggs and had no motive to betray him in such a way.

Others have argued that the ghost ship was fabricated as part of a fake insurance claim. In this theory Morehouse and Briggs are the masterminds behind the abandoned ship. While possible it is unlikely. Neither owned the Mary Celeste and would not have benefited from any insurance claim- at the time James Winchester was the owner.

Even if Winchester was involved in the proposed insurance scam the value of the Mary Celeste and its cargo was fairly modest. In short for this theory to be correct it would mean an awful lot of work for not a lot of money.

A more plausible theory is that the Mary Celeste was the victim of a heavy storm. When the Dei Gratia boarded the stricken ship they found a lot of water in between the decks and a further three and a half foot of water in the hold. Two of the ships water pumps were found to be disassembled leaving only one working pump.

This theory proposes that the Mary Celeste was hit by a severe storm and, thinking he was in charge of a sinking ship, Captain Briggs ordered the crew to abandon ship.

Undermining this theory is that no storms were reported in that part of the Atlantic Ocean during the time the Mary Celeste was at sea. Also the water level was not enough for an experienced captain to abandon ship. The Mary Celeste was still sea worthy. If the crew had intentionally abandoned ship why,

when they realized the ship was safe, did
they not return?

Maybe the crew had abandoned the ship
during a heavy storm and, due to strong
winds and choppy waters, was subsequently
unable to row their lifeboat back to the Mary
Celeste. But if this was the case why was no
trace of the life boat ever found, either in the
busy shipping lanes off the Portuguese coast
or washed up somewhere?

A probable explanation, if we discount the
mysteries of the Bermuda Triangle, lies in the
empty barrels of alcohol which were found
on board. All the empty barrels were made
of red oak; the remaining full barrels were
made of white oak. Red oak is generally
more porous than white oak. The owner of

the Mary Celeste, James Winchester, suggested that there may have been slow leakage through the red oak barrels.

This leakage would have created an alcohol vapor in the hold. As the barrels, which were tied together with steel bands, rubbed against each other the friction generated could have created a spark leading to an explosion.

Witnessing a violent gush of fumes and flame Captain Briggs may have panicked and ordered an immediate abandonment of the ship. In their hurry the crew could have neglected to tie their lifeboat to the ship. In such circumstances a strong wind would have been enough to blow them off course. The crew and Briggs' family would then have drowned or died from hunger or exposure.

The caveat to this theory is that when the crew of the Dei Gratia boarded the Mary Celeste nobody reported smelling alcohol fumes or recorded seeing any burn marks.

Since being found adrift the story of the Mary Celeste has sailed into legend. The story of the ghost ship found drifting off the Portuguese coast is story which has been told and retold numerous times. Whatever the truth about what happened on board, the Mary Celeste is probably one of the most well-known incidents which has been, albeit tenuously, attributed to the Bermuda Triangle.

The Strange Encounter of the Ellen Austin

Many of the earliest disappearances attributed to the Bermuda Triangle involved maritime traffic. One of the more fascinating of these early stories is that of the Ellen Austin.

Built in 1854 in Damariscotta, Maine for the Tucker family of Wiscasset, Maine, the Ellen Austin was a 210 foot long three masted schooner. When finished it weighed 1,812 tons. The schooner was made of white oak.

In early 1855 when sailing from Damariscotta, Maine to Savannah, Georgia the Ellen Austin encountered another ship, the Florence which had lost its mast in a severe gale. Captain Wood and the crew of the Florence were rescued by the Ellen Austin and taken to Savannah.

Later that same year the Ellen Austin departed Savannah for Liverpool. On board was 2,397,817 pounds of cotton. According to the 26th of May, 1855 edition of the Raleigh Register this was the "largest cargo of cotton ever cleared at that port."

By the following year the Ellen Austin was serving as a packet ship for the Patriotic Line. Under the stewardship of Captain William H. Garrick the schooner ran between Liverpool and New York City. This period in the Ellen Austin's career was not the most distinguished.

In July 1856 the Ellen Austin reportedly lost an estimated $60,000 worth of cargo. Meanwhile in February of 1857 reports emerged accusing Captain Garrick and his crew of torture and abuse. One report from the New York Tribune, titled "Brutality at Sea", described how Garrick "knocked [Thomas Campbell] down with a heavy wire rope" before proceeding to "beat him over the back and shoulders". Not satisfied Garrick proceeded to set "two large, ferocious dogs" on Campbell, "who tore and mutilated his legs."

Despite suggestions that Garrick was to be arrested and tried on these accusations it seems that this did not happen. In August 1857 Garrick was still in charge of the Ellen Austin. By now the ownership of the Ellen

Austin had passed to Hamilton and Graham. For the next few years the she continued to carry passengers and cargo between Liverpool and New York.

In 1867 the route of the Ellen Austin changed and it began to sail from New York to San Francisco. Over the next few years the ship was involved in a number of collisions and suffered further damage in heavy gales and storms.

By 1874 the Ellen Austin had been fully repaired and was under the command of the elderly Captain A. J. Griffin. She was now sailing under the colors of Grinnell, Minturn and Company's Red Swallowtail Line of London.

Once again the Ellen Austin was sailing between New York and London. It was during one of its final journeys for the Swallowtail Line that the Ellen Austin made a discovery that would launch it into the history books.

Having departed London for New York in December 1880 the Ellen Austin was several weeks into its journey when it came across an unidentified schooner drifting aimlessly just north of the Sargasso Sea. (The Sargasso Sea is at the heart of the Bermuda Triangle.)

Suspicious Captain Baker ordered the Ellen Austin's crew to follow and observe the schooner for a few days in case it was a trap. After two days of no activity of movement Captain Baker decided that it was safe to move closer. The Ellen Austin moved within hailing distance.

Getting no response Captain Baker gathered four of his men and rowed towards the abandoned ship. Still unable to get a response Captain Baker ordered his men to draw weapons and to follow him on board. Despite an expectation that they were walking into an ambush the men found that they were, unexpectedly, alone.

An inspection of the schooner showed it to be shipshape and in a well-maintained condition. There was no sign of violence but there was also no sign of the crew.

Along with the schooners crew Captain Baker found that the ship's log and its nameplates, which should have been attached to the bow, were missing. An inspection of the ship's hold found that it contained a shipment of mahogany. This led Baker to speculate that the schooner had possibly been sailing from Honduras to either and an English or a Mediterranean port. Baker assigned some of his most trusted men to man the ship and to follow the Ellen Austin to New York.

Within a matter of hours both schooners were under way. For the next two days things seemed to be normal. As the waters were calm they were able to sail within earshot of each other. This changed on the third day when they were separated by a fierce Atlantic storm- a side effect of a hurricane tearing through Alabama,

Mississippi and Georgia. By the time the storm abated a few days later the ships had lost contact.

When the skies cleared and the seas calmed visibility became excellent, extending for miles. The water was as flat as a mirror. Despite these excellent conditions, and much to the bewilderment of Captain Baker and the crew of the Ellen Austin, the second schooner was nowhere to be seen. Ordering his lookouts to remain alert Captain Baker ordered the Ellen Austin to continue on its course.

After a while one of Baker's lookouts spotted the schooner. Through his spyglass Captain Baker could see the sails of the ship. He could also tell that once again it seemed to be drifting aimlessly through the ocean. Baker ordered the Ellen Austin change its course in order to intercept the schooner for a second time. The second ship was sailing so erratically that it took a few hours for the Ellen Austin to catch her.

As the Ellen Austin closed in on the schooner Captain Baker and the crew attempted to hail the ship. No answer came. As before Captain Baker assembled a boarding party and, fully armed, made his way to the schooner.

In a scene eerily reminiscent of their first boarding of the schooner Baker and his men once again found no sign of a crew. The cargo hold remained full but the beds weren't slept in and the food rations appeared untouched. The new log book Captain Baker had sent over with the new crew was also missing. It was as if the first encounter between the Ellen Austin and the mystery schooner had never happened.

Captain Baker now faced opposition from his crew, some of whom believed that the schooner was cursed and wished to abandon it at sea. Not a naturally superstitious man Captain Baker remained keen to capitalize on the potential salvage opportunity of a ship in good working order. While he didn't know what had happened to the crew he thought it unlikely it could happen again.

So it was that Captain Baker spent the next few hours trying to convince the superstitious sailors of the Ellen Austin to man the schooner. Despite his belief that there was probably a rational explanation behind the disappearances his crew was equally convinced that there was something evil at work on the seas. With the promise of close contact and firearms a second crew was eventually convinced to undertake the task of sailing the schooner to New York.

As the second crew readied the schooner to set sail the clear skies were replaced by a dense fog which settled ominously on the water, reducing visibility to a couple of feet. Once again the Ellen Austin lost sight of the schooner.

When the fog finally lifted the second schooner was nowhere to be seen. Unnerved

Captain Baker and the Ellen Austin hurriedly set sail for New York.

The Ellen Austin would never see the schooner or its missing crew again. Soon after arriving in New York she was sold to a German company and re-named the Meta. The Meta was reportedly wrecked whilst sailing along the American coast in 1883 under the command of Captain A. J. Griffin.

After the Meta's demise the story of the Ellen Austin's encounter would, like the mystery schooner, disappear. Sporadically different versions of the tale of the Ellen Austin would be retold by various sources over the next few decades.

It resurfaced in various reports in 1906 and again, as a radio broadcast by retired British Naval office Lieutenant Commander Rupert T. Gould, in 1935. With each retelling some details would change- sometimes the date, sometimes the Ellen Austin's destination.

So how much of the story of the Ellen Austin's strange encounter is true?

As there are so few documented details about the Ellen Austin's encounter knowing the exact details is extremely difficult. We know for sure that there was a ship called the Ellen Austin which sailed between London and New York.

That she left London for New York on the 5th of December 1880 is also an undeniable fact, however at that time she was under the command of Captain A. J. Griffin not Captain Baker. We also know for certain that by 1881 the Ellen Austin had been renamed Meta and was sailing under the colors of a German company.

The area sailed by the Ellen Austin north of the Sargasso Sea was an area well known for derelict ships. Any craft abandoned south of this point would be drawn north by the currents before being caught in the particular drifts and tides of the Sargasso Sea. Derelict ships drifting out of the Bermuda Triangle would often be found in this area. Indeed the Ellen Austin had previously found other derelict ships here.

We also know that the Ellen Austin did not arrive in New York until February 1881. As she had set sail at the start of December this seems an unusually long time for her to make the crossing. The time spent chasing the mystery schooner would account for this considerable delay.

While all the stories of the Ellen Austin have some discrepancies they also all agree on certain facts. Notably that there was no sign of a struggle, the food and munitions supplies were plentiful and that the cargo hold was full. This adds a little credence to the story of the abandoned schooner.

For sceptics that there is little in the way of documented evidence suggests that the story is little more than a work of fiction. Little of the story was reported in the press at the time and despite the numerous witnesses we have no witness testimony from the crew of the Ellen Austin.

Instead the story has been passed from sailor to sailor, growing with each retelling. We also have no reports of schooners carrying a cargo of mahogany going missing; this is assuming that the schooner was acting properly before it befell its initial misfortune.

It is possible that while the story has been exaggerated in the retelling the basic facts of it- that a schooner called the Ellen Austin discovered an abandoned ship and despite attempting to bring it to port for salvage lost her due to inclement weather, seem plausible.

What happened to the crew of this schooner, and any subsequent men left by the Ethel Austin to pilot the schooner be it accident, foul play or the mysteries of the Bermuda Triangle will never be known.

The Disappearance of the U.S.S. Cyclops

The U.S.S. Cyclops was one of four Proteus class cargo ships built for the U.S. Navy in the years before World War One. Launched on the 7th of May 1910 from the yards of William Cramp and Sons, Philadelphia the U.S.S. Cyclops was named for the Cyclops from Greek mythology. She was the second U.S. Naval vessel to bear the name.

The U.S.S. Cyclops entered service on the 7th of November 1910. Lieutenant Commander George Worley of the Naval Auxiliary Service was at the helm.

Between May and July 1911 the U.S.S. Cyclops operated with the Naval Auxiliary

Service, Atlantic Fleet sailing in the Baltic seas. Its role was to supply Second Division ships. After returning to Norfolk, Virginia the Cyclops operated on the east coast-sailing between Newport, Rhode Island and the Caribbean, servicing the fleet. The U.S.S. Cyclops continued to supply the fleet and aided in the evacuation of refugees during the 1914- 1915 American occupation of Veracruz, Mexico.

Following the American entry into World War One the U.S.S. Cyclops was commissioned on the 1st of May 1917. Lieutenant Commander George W. Worley remained in command. The Cyclops was part of a convoy which sailed for Saint-Nazaire, France in June 1917. She returned to the U.S. the following month.

With the exception of a mission to Halifax, Nova Scotia, the U.S.S. Cyclops served predominantly on the east coast until early in January 1918. She was then assigned to the Naval Overseas Transportation service. Here she was tasked with supplying fuel to British ships in the south Atlantic. During this period the U.S.S. Cyclops and its crew were praised on various occasions for their part in the war effort.

On the 16th of February 1918 the U.S.S. Cyclops left port at Rio de Janeiro sailing for Bahia. When she arrived here on the 20th of February Worley submitted a report concerning the starboard engine- a cylinder had cracked and it was inoperative. It was decided to delay repairs to the ship until it returned to the United States.

The 18th of February saw the U.S.S. Cyclops set sail for Baltimore. Its route would take it through the heart of the infamous Bermuda Triangle.

The sailing to Baltimore was intended to be a direct sailing with no scheduled stops however the Cyclops docked in Barbados on the 3rd of March. Here Worley visited Charles Ludlow Livingston, the United States consul, while the ship took on additional cargo.

Barbadian port officials reported that this led to water reaching over the Cyclops' Plimsoll line suggesting that the ship was overloaded. Ignoring the concerns of the port officials the Cyclops left Barbados for Baltimore on the 4th of March.

Five days later on the 9th of March a molasses tanker, the Amalco, sighted the U.S.S. Cyclops near Virginia. This was to be the last ever sighting of the ship. The following day a violent storm swept through the Virginia Cape region.

The U.S.S. Cyclops never reached its intended destination of Baltimore. Despite an extensive search the U.S.S. Cyclops was never seen or heard from again and three months later was officially declared lost.

According to some sources in 1968 a Navy diver reported the discovery of the wreck of an old ship off the Norfolk Virginia coast. After looking at pictures the diver later identified it as the U.S.S. Cyclops. The location he was diving was roughly the area where the Cyclops was last seen.

Could the Cyclops overloaded and suffering from engine trouble have simply been sunk in a violent storm? Further expeditions to the site have failed to find the wreckage.

For some the solution is simple: a combination of a violent storm and an overloaded ship with engine trouble caused the loss of the U.S.S. Cyclops. Others see something more sinister in the ships disappearance.

Just as the official search of the Cyclops was finishing a telegram was sent to the U.S. State department from Charles Ludlow Livingston, the United States consul in

Barbados. The telegram stated claimed that Captain Worley was referred to by the crew as the "damned Dutchman" and was disliked by the other officers.

Livingston claimed that there were rumors of men being confined and one even being executed. He also suggested that there were numerous Germanic names amongst the crew.

An investigation by Naval Intelligence revealed that Captain Worley had been born Johan Frederick Wichmann in Sandstedt, Hanover, Germany in 1862. He had entered America by jumping ship in San Francisco in 1878.

By 1898 Wichmann had changed his named to Worley and was operating a saloon in San Francisco's Barbary Coast. During this period he qualified for the position of ship's master and commanded several civilian merchant ships. These ships delivered cargo between the Far East to San Francisco, not always legally.

Report from the crew who served under Worley suggested that he was not an easy man to sail with, often berating them for trivial matters. This didn't stop Worley being commissioned as a lieutenant commander in the Naval Auxiliary Reserve on the 21st of February 1917.

Naval Intelligence found that Worley's eccentric behavior continued after his commission. There were even reports of violence; on one occasion he reportedly chased an ensign around the ship with a pistol. Worley also had a habit of putting an inexperienced officer in charge of loading cargo while more experienced men were confined to quarters.

It was this practice that had led to the U.S.S. Cyclops being dangerously overloaded on her final voyage and may have ultimately led to her sinking. But not even this is the most damming accusation which was levelled against Worley. Many accused him of being pro-German and suggested that he had colluded with the enemy.

It is true that his closest friends and associates were Germans or Americans of

German descent. Indeed Livingston speculated that many of those on board the Cyclops were German sympathizers.

A passenger on board the Cyclops was Alfred Louis Moreau Gottschalk the consul general in Rio de Janeiro. Gottschalk, like Worley was known to have pro- German sympathies. Charles Ludlow Livingston believed, according to his telegram, that Gottschalk and Worley had collaborated in handing the ship over to the Germans. After the conclusion of World War One a check of the German records found no sign of the Cyclops.

Today the disappearance of the U.S.S. Cyclops remains the largest loss of life on a ship not involved in combat. With no firm evidence for the fate of the U.S.S. Cyclops many have credited its disappearance to the Bermuda triangle. The case of the Cyclops is considered by many to be one of the Bermuda Triangle's best documented cases.

The Mystery of the Carroll A. Deering

The Carroll A. Deering was a large five masted schooner. It measured around 255 feet long and was over 44 foot wide. It weighed around 1,879 tons. In 1921 the Carroll A. Deering was found run aground in mysterious circumstances off the coast of North Carolina. No trace of its crew was ever found.

The mystery of the Carroll A. Deering is attributed to the Bermuda Triangle because it passed through a long stretch of the Triangle on its final fateful journey.

The Carroll A. Deering was built in the shipyard in Maine, New England in 1919 by the G.G. Deering Company. The owner of the company, G. G. Deering, named the ship after his son Carroll. It was the latest addition to a fleet of about 100 ships. The Carroll A. Deering had been in use as a cargo ship for just over a year when it embarked on its final voyage.

On the final journey the Carroll A. Deering was to be captained by William H. Merritt. He was also a part owner of the ship. Using this position he employed his 29 year old son as first mate. The nine other crew members, all Scandinavians, were selected quickly; their identities and histories are largely unknown.

In late August of 1921 the Carroll A. Deering set sail. After leaving port in Boston, Captain

Merritt fell seriously ill. Unable to continue on the journey the ship diverted to the port at Lewes, Delaware.

Here Captain Merritt left the ship. His son also disembarked, intending to take care of his sick father. Both men were to have a lucky escape.

A new captain, 66 year old veteran of the sea's Captain W. B. Wormell took charge. A second man, Charles B. McLellan also boarded the ship in Delaware. McLellan was to act as first mate. With the crew replete the Carroll A. Deering set sail for Rio de Janeiro. It reached its destination on the 8th of September 1921.

Despite this leg of the journey appearing to be a smooth sailing in reality this was not the case. Tensions between the crew became apparent after the ship reached Rio de Janeiro.

It was here that Captain Wormell met his old friend Captain Goodwin. Goodwin later reported that Wormell had sounded concerned when he talked about the crew of the Carroll A. Deering.

Wormell had apparently taken a dislike to First Mate McLellan thinking he was useless and a trouble maker. Both Captain Goodwin and Captain Wormell agreed that the first engineer, Herbert Bates, was efficient and could be relied on should any problems arise. (Captain Goodwin knew Bates well having sailed with him previously.)

On the 2nd of December 1921 the Carroll A. Deering set sail on its return journey. When the ship docked in Barbados an inebriated first mate McLellan was reported to have complained about Captain Wormell to a Captain Norton and his first mate. McLellan suggested that he had to do all the navigation due to Wormell's poor eyesight. McLellan also claimed that he often found himself having to control the crew who were frequently restless and unsettled due to Wormell's interference.

Later that night Captain Norton along with other members of his crew claimed to have heard McLellan shouting that he would kill

Captain Wormell before their voyage was over. McLellan was arrested in drunken state.

The next day Captain Wormell generously ensured that McLellan was released without charge from the lock up. McLellan rejoined the ship and on January 9th 1921, Carroll A. Deering set sail from Barbados to their home port of Portland, Maine.

At some point after setting sail from Barbados, as the ship sailed through an area of the Bermuda Triangle, things went wrong. On the 29th of January the Carroll A. Deering was spotted by a lightship at Cape Lookout, North Carolina.

The Captain of the lightship, Captain Jacobson, heard a crewman from Carroll A. Deering hailing him, saying they had lost their anchors and this information needed to be reported to the parent company G. G. Deering. However the Carroll A. Deering did not stop and continued on its course.

Captain Jacobson recorded that the man on the Carroll A. Deering did not look or sound like the captain or the first mate, rather he looked like a member of the crew. He also noticed that several other crewmen were gathering at the fore deck of the ship which was quite unusual as the crew is not usually allowed to access that area. This was the last sighting of the Carroll A. Deering manned and in a seemingly normal condition.

A few hours after this incident a second steamer passed the lightship. It had no name or means of identification. As the radio on the lightship was out of order Jacobson blew the lightship's whistle, trying to catch the attention of the steamer. The whistle was powerful enough to be heard 5 miles away but the steamer paid it no heed. It kept on moving in the same direction as Carroll A. Deering.

Two days later, on the thirty first of January 1921 the Carroll A. Deering was found aground at Diamond Shoals. This is an area off the coast of Cape Hatteras, North Carolina and is fringed with reefs.

Due to the harsh sea conditions the coast guards were unable to approach the stricken ship immediately. It wasn't until the morning of the fourth of February did they finally manager to board the Carroll A. Deering.

When the coast guard boarded the ship they were met with an eerie sight. The Carroll A. Deering was completely abandoned. In the galley food was found in the process of being prepared which suggested that the abandonment happened in a hurry. Several things, including two lifeboats, were missing.

All the papers and documents including the log, and carious navigational instruments were also absent. Meanwhile an inspection of the Captain's cabin turned up several pairs of boots which suggested that more people than just the captain had been using the room.

Another strange discovery was a string of red lights which were found to be running up the mast. This suggested that someone had been trying to send a signal to someone or something else. The ship's main anchors were also missing.

A large map on a ship is used to record the day to day route and movement. When the coast guard inspected the Carroll A. Deering's map they noted that Captain Wormell had been marking the map until the 23rd of January. After that date someone else's handwriting marked the map.

After the coast guard completed their investigation attempts were made to tow the Carroll A. Deering away. These all failed and it was eventually deemed that the ship was unable to be saved. In its position at Diamond Shoals it was also considered a danger to other ships. On the 4th of March 1921 the wreck of the Carroll A. Deering was sunk using dynamite.

There are numerous theories concerning the fate of the Carroll A. Deering.

The most popular is that of a plotted rebellion by the crew members, led by the first mate McLellan. Ostensibly this seems like the most acceptable theory. It was evident from Captain Wormell's comments at Rio de Janeiro that he didn't trust his first mate and was not comfortable with other members of the crew. McLellan's actions in Barbados also add weight to this theory.

This theory seems plausible and the strange actions of the crew as they passed the lightship would suggest that the captain had been displaced. The disappearance of the crew could then be put down to a move to avoid the inevitable inquiry and trail.

McLellan and the others would have lived out the remainder of their lives under assumed identities. However if McLellan had lead a mutiny would he have so brazenly sailed past the light ship?

During the days of prohibition smuggling wine and spirits using stolen cargo ships was a common practice. The second ship reported by the light ship which lacked any form of identification fits the profile of one of these "rum runners". Some investigators have proposed that this second steamer did not stop because it was carrying illegal liquor.

While trying to drop the liquor somewhere along the coastline this second ship could have come across the Carroll A. Deering. In order to eliminate all witnesses those on board the second ship may have killed the crew of the Carroll A. Deering.

In a similar vein some argue that the Carroll A. Deering was stolen during its return journey by a group of rum runners who were operating out of Bahamas. They used the ship to smuggle spirits into America before abandoning it. It was a well-known fact that the Carroll A. Deering had a huge hold which could easily store large quantities of valuable illicit alcohol.

That the Carroll A Deering was so easily identifiable and quite slow means that it was an unlikely target for smugglers looking to appropriate a boat.

Like the smuggling theory the suggestion that the Carroll A. Deering was the victim of pirates seems unlikely. While piracy was common in the area at the time, indeed the widow of Captain Wormell firmly believed this to be the cause of her husband's disappearance, there is no firm evidence to support it.

The United States weather department has long held the belief that hurricanes were the cause of the Carroll A. Deering's misfortune. At least nine other vessels disappeared or met with fatal accidents in the same area during this period in early 1921 due to hurricanes.

The S.S. Hewitt, a Sulphur carrier, was geographically close to the Carroll A. Deering during this late January period. Indeed some claim that the unnamed steamer which passed by the lightship at Cape Lookout and never stopped was the SS Hewitt.

When the S.S. Hewitt failed to arrive in Boston on its expected date at the end of January a search was launched. No trace of the ship was ever found. The theory that both the Carroll A. Deering and S.S. Hewitt were victims of a hurricane is undermined evidence which shows the two ships were moving out of the storm affected area and were therefore unlikely to have been affected by a hurricane.

With no better theory the fate of the crew of the Carroll A. Deering, and the S.S. Hewitt, remains unsolved. Many claim they are just two more victims of the infamous Bermuda Triangle.

The Disappearance of Flight 19

When selecting its victims the Bermuda Triangle does not confine itself to sea going crafts. Many aircrafts have also been affected. One of the most famous aviation mysteries is that of Flight 19.

Flight 19 was the designation of five Grumman TBM Avenger torpedo bombers that departed from Naval Air Station Fort Lauderdale, Florida on the 5th of December 1945. It disappeared during what was supposed to be a routine training run through an area of the Bermuda Triangle.

Naval Air Station Fort Lauderdale was an airfield operated by the United States Navy located just outside Fort Lauderdale, Florida. Since 1942 it had been used as a base for training pilots and enlisted aircrew (gunners, radio operators etc.). These men were trained to operate Grumman Avenger torpedo bombers.

The base was also used to train ground crew such as those tasked with aircraft maintenance. Among the Avenger pilots who trained at Fort Lauderdale was former President George H. W. Bush who graduated in 1943.

Training was difficult and dangerous. Between 1942 and 1946 ninety four men lost their lives whilst serving at Fort Lauderdale. Fourteen of these men were on board the five Avengers which made up Flight 19.

On the 5th of December 1945 Flight 19 undertook a routine navigation and combat training exercise commonly known on the base as "Navigation problem No 1". This was a combination of bombing and navigation. Flight 19 was not the first nor was it the last training group to tackle Navigation problem No 1 that day.

The flight leader was Lieutenant Charles Carroll Taylor. He had around 2,500 flying hours in Avenger type aircraft and had recently completed a combat tour of the Pacific. During this tour Taylor had served as a torpedo bomber pilot on the aircraft carrier U.S.S. Hancock. Following that he had spent some time as a VTB instructor at N.A.S. Miami. In short Taylor was an experienced pilot.

Taylor's role on Flight 19 was to be one of supervisor with a trainee pilot taking over responsibilities for leading the flight. Should anything go wrong then Taylor would be on hand to step in. Taylor's trainee pilots each had 300 hours total and 60 flight hours in the Avenger.

The men, U.S. marine Captains Edward Joseph Powers and George William Stivers, U.S. Marine Second Lieutenant Forrest James Gerber and U.S.N. Ensign Joseph Tipton Bossi; had recently completed other training missions in the area where the training flight was scheduled to take place. The remainders of the men making up Flight 19 were either trainee gunners or radiomen.

Flying with Taylor were gunner George Devlin and radio operator Walter R. Parpart. On board with Captain Powers were gunner Sergeant Howell O. Thompson and radioman Sergeant George R. Paonessa. Accompanying Captain Stivers were Sergeant Robert F. Gallivan, gunner, and private radio operator Robert R. Gruebel. Gunner Herman A. Thelander and radioman Burt E. Baulk were on board Ensign Joseph Bossi's flight.

The final aircraft that of Second Lieutenant Gerber was one crewman short. Corporal Allan Kosnar had asked to be excused from the exercise. This left only gunner William E. Lightfoot on board with Gerber.

Before takeoff the aircraft were all filled with fuel and underwent the usual pre- flight checks. At this point it was discovered that all five of the Avengers were missing clocks. As the purpose of the flight was to teach the principles of dead reckoning (the process of calculating one's position by using a previously determined position and advancing that position based upon known or estimated speeds over elapsed time and course) this was not a major concern. It was also assumed that each man had his own watch.

Flight 19's take off was delayed from 13:45 to 14:10 as Taylor was late arriving. As the five Avengers prepared to take off the weather at N.A.S. Fort Lauderdale was described as "favorable, sea state moderate to rough."

"Navigation problem No. 1" involved three different legs however Flight 19 was scheduled to fly four legs. After takeoff Flight 19 flew on a heading of 091° (almost due east) for 56 nautical miles until reaching Hen and Chickens Shoals. Here low level bombing practice was carried out.

The flight was to then continue on the same heading for other 67nautical miles before turning onto a course of 346° for 73nautical miles. During this leg the flight was to fly over Grand Bahama Island. Its next scheduled turn was to a heading of 241° where they would fly for 120nautical miles completing the exercise. Flight 19 was to then return to Fort Lauderdale.

Thanks to radio conversation between the pilots which was overheard by both Fort Lauderdale other aircraft in the area we known that the practice bombing operation was completed. At about 15:00 a pilot requested and was given permission to drop his last bomb.

Forty minutes later, another flight instructor, Lieutenant Robert F. Cox in a FT-74, was forming up with his group of students in preparation for undertaking the same mission when he received an unidentified transmission.

An unidentified crew member of Flight 19 asked Powers, one of Flight 19's trainee pilots, for his compass reading. Powers replied: "I don't know where we are. We must have got lost after that last turn."

Over his radio Lieutenant Cox identified himself before asking Powers to identify himself so that he could be given assistance. Cox's message was seemingly not heard by Powers as no response was given. Instead others in Flight 19 began to respond to Powers making suggestions.

Cox tried again, and finally made contact with Taylor. Taylor informed Cox that both his compasses were out and that he was having trouble finding Fort Lauderdale. Taylor reported that he was "over land but it's broken. I am sure I'm in the Keys but I don't know how far down and I don't know how to get to Fort Lauderdale."

Cox informed the N.A.S. Fort Lauderdale that Taylor's flight was lost before advising Taylor to put the sun on his port wing and fly north up the coast to Fort Lauderdale.

While Cox tried to advice Taylor Fort Lauderdale was trying to establish if any of the Avengers in Flight 19 were equipped with a transmitter. The hope was that they could use this to triangulate the flight's position. Taylor didn't respond to Fort Lauderdale's questions but would later indicate that his transmitter was activated.

Instead Taylor radioed to say that Flight 19 was "heading 030 degrees for 45 minutes, then we will fly north to make sure we are not over the Gulf of Mexico." This was at 16:45. During this time no bearings could be made on the flight, and their transmitters could not be picked up.

Taylor did not respond to an order to switch his radio frequency to broadcast on 4805 kHz. When ordered to switch to 3000 kHz, the search and rescue frequency, Taylor refused saying that "I cannot switch frequencies. I must keep my planes intact."

At 16:56, Taylor was again asked to turn on his transmitter. Taylor did not acknowledge this but a few minutes later advised his flight "Change course to 090 degrees (due east) for 10 minutes." At the same time another member of Flight 19 was heard to say "Dammit, if we could just fly west we would get home; head west, dammit." That the students didn't, if they believed this to be the case, break off and head west of their own accord had been attributed to military discipline.

As the weather deteriorated, radio contact became intermittent. Those on the ground at Fort Lauderdale began to think that Flight 19 was more than 200nautical miles out to sea east of the Florida peninsula. At 17:24 Taylor radioed his intention to "fly 270 degrees west until landfall or running out of gas" and requested a weather check.

By 17:50 several land based radio stations had triangulated Flight 19's position as being north of the Bahamas and well off the coast of central Florida, but nobody transmitted this information on an open, repetitive basis.

At 18:04, Taylor was heard to radio to the rest of Flight 19 "holding 270, we didn't fly far enough east, we may as well just turn around and fly east again". By that time, the weather had deteriorated even more and the sun had set. At around 18:20 Taylor's last message was received. (Some accounts claim that Taylor's last message was received at 19:04.)

Taylor was heard to say "all planes close up tight ... we'll have to ditch unless landfall ... when the first plane drops below 10 gallons, we all go down together." This was the last anyone ever heard from the stricken Flight 19.

As it became obvious that Flight 19 was lost Fort Lauderdale alerted all air bases, aircraft, and merchant ships in the area. A consolidated PBY Catalina was sent to locate Flight 19 and guide them back to base, leaving Fort Lauderdale shortly after 18:00.

After dark two Martin PBM Mariner flying boats originally scheduled for their own training flights were diverted to perform square pattern searches in an area west of 29°N 79°W.

One of these PBM Martin Mariners took off from Naval Air Station Banana River (now known as Patrick Air Force Base). Lieutenant Walter G. Jeffery USN was piloting the flight. Also on board were Lieutenant Harrie G. Cone USN, Ensign Roger M. Allen USN, Ensign Lloyd A. Eliason USN, Ensign Charles D. Arceneaux USN, radioman

Robert C. Cameron USN, Seaman Wiley D. Cargill USN, James F. Jordan USN, John T. Menendez USN, seaman Philip B. Neeman USN, James F. Osterheld USN, Donald E. Peterson USN and seaman Alfred J. Zywicki USN. After calling in a routine radio message at 19:30 Lieutenant Jeffrey and the Martin Mariner was never heard from again.

Both Martin Mariners were in the best of conditions so engine failure was ruled out as was an accidental explosion caused by someone smoking on board. Interestingly the Navy board of investigation into the disappearance of Flight 19 reported that greenish lights were often seen along the Florida coast lines. The lights would float around for a while before disappearing slowly. This phenomenon is often linked to St Elmo's fire.

This light is caused due to the areas unique climate and radiates a hue electrical charge. It is also known that aeroplanes can appear to glow green when they come under the charge from Saint Elmo's fire even though they have anti-static equipment. On one such occasion this has caused a plane to explode.

So did Saint Elmo's fire lead to the loss of the Martin Mariner or did the Bermuda Triangle claiming yet another victim on that December night in 1941?

At 21:15 the tanker S.S. Gaines Mills reported observing flames from an apparent explosion leaping 100feet in the air and burning for 10 minutes. The reported position of these flames was 28°N 80.25°W. The S.S. Gaines Mills' Captain S. Stanley unsuccessfully searched for survivors through a pool of oil and aviation gasoline.

The escort carrier U.S.S. Solomons reported losing radar contact with an aircraft at the same position and time. While this is unlikely to have been Flight 19 it is possible that the S.S. Gaines Mills and U.S.S. Solomons witnessed the final moments of the Martin Mariner.

So what became of Flight 19? A few months later the Navy board of investigation published a 500 page report. In it they observed that Taylor had mistakenly believed the small islands he had passed over were the Florida Keys.

If the islands were the Keys then Flight 19 was over the Gulf of Mexico and heading north east would have taken them to Florida, reaching landfall in roughly twenty minutes.

A later reconstruction of the incident showed that the islands visible to Taylor were probably the Bahamas. These are well north east of the Keys. The board of investigation found that because of Taylor's belief that he was on a base course toward Florida, Taylor actually guided the flight farther north east and out to sea.

It was generally accepted at N.A.S. Fort Lauderdale that if a pilot ever became lost in the area to fly a heading of 270° west (or in evening hours toward the sunset). By the time Flight 19 turned west they were probably so far out to sea that they didn't have enough fuel to reach land. This combined with bad weather, and the ditching characteristics of the Avenger, meant that there was little hope of rescue even if they had managed to stay afloat.

It has also been suggested that Flight 19 overshot Castaway Cay and reached another land mass in the southern Abaco Islands. They then preceded North West as planned fully expecting to see the Grand Bahama Island in front of them.

Instead they saw the northern part of Abaco Island on their right. If Taylor had incorrectly assumed that this was the Grand Bahama Island and that his compass was malfunctioning the flight would have set a course of south west back to Fort Lauderdale. In reality this course would have taken them further North West into the open ocean.

Adding to this confusion as Flight 19 embarked on their incorrect path they would have encountered a series of islands north of Abaco Island. These resemble the Key West Islands and would have confirmed to mistaken Flight 19 that they were on the correct course. The Fort Lauderdale control tower telling Flight 19 to fly west, which should have brought them to Florida, would have really sent the flight north west on a path almost parallel to Florida.

After flying west for a while and still believing that they were near Key West Taylor would have realized that they should have reached land. The control tower informing Flight 19 that they were not in the Key West area led to further confusion.

Some of the aircraft in the flight believed that their compasses were working- Taylor by this point didn't trust his. If Flight 19 were above Key West flying on a north east bearing according to their compasses would have taken them to Florida.

When this failed Flight 19 would have flown west, which should have taken them to Florida if they were above Bahama. If they had maintained this course they would have reached some form of land before running out of fuel.

However Taylor, deciding that they had gone far enough West and that they were near Key West after all, set Flight 19 on a course north east. This would have seen them running out of fuel and crashing into the ocean off the east coast of Florida, north of Abaco Island.

The Navy board of investigation report originally laid the blame for the disappearance of Flight 19 on Taylor. Deeming him ultimately responsible for the series of navigational errors. The report was later amended to show "cause unknown" after a campaign by Taylor's mother who contended that the Navy was unfairly blaming her son for the loss of five aircraft and 14 men, when the Navy had neither the bodies nor the aircraft as evidence.

In 1986, while searching for the wreckage of the Space Shuttle Challenger, the wreckage of an Avenger was found off the Florida coast. Despite an initial belief that it was one of the Avengers from Flight 19 when aviation archaeologist Jon Myhre raised this wreck from the ocean floor in 1990 it was found not to be one of the planes.

In 1991, a treasure-hunting expedition led by Graham Hawkes announced that the wreckage of five Avengers had been discovered off the coast of Florida. Hawkes still believes this to be Flight 19. After cross checking the tail numbers it was revealed that these were not Flight 19.

It was later established that an Avenger had been lost at sea on the 9th of October 1943 (its crew all survived). Despite the odds it was concluded that this was just a random collection of accidents that happened to rest in the same area.

Today some see the disappearance of Flight 19 as a tragic accident caused by a series of navigational errors. For others the malfunctioning compasses, strange lights and lack of wreckage suggest that Flight 19 and the Martin Mariner are just two more victims of the Bermuda Triangle.

The Disappearance of the Douglas DC-3

On the night of December the 28th 1948, near the end of a scheduled flight from Puerto Rica to Miami a Douglas DC-3 disappeared with 31 people on board. Their flight would take them straight through the Bermuda Triangle.

As Captain Robert Linquist prepared for what he expected to be a routine flight from Puerto Rica to Miami he went through all the usual checks. On finding that the aircraft batteries were discharged Linquist was unconcerned. He assumed that they would be recharged by the aircraft's generators en route.

Unwilling to delay the aircraft's scheduled take off time and keen to take advantage of the predicted good weather Linquist decided to press ahead with the flight.

Despite the dying batteries the Douglas DC-3 seemed to be in good order. Since becoming operational in 1936 it had a total of 28,257 flying hours prior to the 28th of December 1948. It had been inspected several times over the previous two years and was certified to be airworthy.

Additionally the aircraft had recently been given a partial overhaul complete with two new engines. It is not for nothing that these planes have a reputation as being amongst the most reliable ever built.

Accompanying Linquist on board that night were his co-pilot Ernest Hill and stewardess Mary Burke. The plane was also carrying 29 passengers. As Linquist taxied to the end of runway 27 the aircrafts three crew and passengers could have no idea of what was to come.

At the end of the runway the Douglas DC-3 stopped. When the aircraft didn't respond to repeated attempts at radio communication from the control tower the head of Puerto Rican Transport drove out to find what was wrong.

Linquist reported that the radio could not transmit because of the low batteries. After some discussion Linquist agreed to stay close to San Juan until the batteries were recharged enough to allow two-way contact. At 22:03 flight NC16002 took to the skies.

After circling the city for 11 minutes the Douglas DC-3's batteries seemed sufficiently recharged. Linquist conversed with the authorities at San Juan over the radio for a few moments. When all was deemed well the flight received permission to proceed to Miami, following the previously submitted flight plan.

This was the last communication that San Juan was to receive from flight NC16002. All further attempts went unanswered.

At 23:23 Miami's Overseas Foreign Air Route Traffic Control Centre heard a routine transmission from Linquist's Douglas DC-3.

The voice, almost certainly Linquist's, reported that the aircraft was at 8,300 feet and their expected time of arrival was 04:03.

This message placed the flight at roughly 700 miles from Miami. Throughout the night Miami would, sporadically, hear other transmissions from Linquist. All seemed routine.

At 04:13 Linquist reported that he was 50 miles south of Miami. If we are to go by Linquist's earlier expected time of arrival then the flight was ten minutes late. While this transmission was not heard at the Overseas Foreign Air Route Traffic Control Centre in Miami it was heard 600 miles away in New Orleans, Louisiana.

The transmission was then relayed by New Orleans to Miami. Later the accident investigation report, issued by the Civil Aeronautics Boards, said that Linquist may have incorrectly reported his position.

Whatever the position of the Douglas DC-3's this message was the last time that anyone was to ever hear from Linquist or flight NC16002. Further attempts by both Miami and New Orleans to contact flight NC16002 proved pointless.

Since the Douglas DC-3 left San Juan the wind direction at Miami had changed from North West to north east. If the Douglas DC-3 had not received messages informing them of this change then the aircraft could have drifted 40 to 50 miles off course.

As a result of this the subsequent search area for flight NC16002 was widened to include hills in Cuba, the Everglades and even waters in the Gulf of Mexico.

Despite the search for flight NC16002 covering an extensive area no trace of the aircraft was ever found. The search parties were not helped in their efforts by the fact that there were no reports of an explosion or of a plane crashing. This has led to the disappearance of the Douglas DC-3 being attributed to the Bermuda Triangle.

Seven days after the Douglas DC-3 disappeared two bodies were found around 52 miles south of Guantanamo Bay, Cuba. The identity of these bodies remains unknown. Despite initial hopes it has never been established that they are connected to flight NC16002.

More recently people diving in the waters of the Bermuda Triangle have reportedly found a plane similar to the missing Douglas DC-3. It is yet to be firmly established whether this is the missing plane.

The subsequent investigation into the Douglas DC-3's disappearance found that the aircraft was airworthy and that all the crew was certified however at the time of take off the aircraft did not meet the requirements of its operating certificate.

The investigation also found that the company's maintenance records were incomplete. While this is a serious error incomplete records alone are not enough to have caused the Douglas DC-3 to crash.

The investigation also found several incidents of human error on the night of the aircraft's disappearance. Linquist was portrayed as negligent for neglecting to have fully charged batteries before taking off.

This was subsequently believed to have affected the Douglas DC-3's ability to communicate via its radio. As the aircrafts radio communication ability had failed it was probably impossible for Miami and New Orleans to inform them of the change in wind direction.

Another minor contributing factor emerged with the discovery that the aircraft had been allowed to take off despite being 118 lbs. above its allowable cargo limit. The aircraft had fuel for seven and a half hours of flight. At the time of their last known transmission the Douglas DC-3 had been in the air for six hours and ten minutes.

This coupled with the extra weight and change in wind direction meant, the investigation concluded, that an "error in location would be critical".

Due to the lack of wreckage and with it the absence of various key pieces of information the cause for the loss of the flight NC16002 has never been firmly established. Some see it as a simple case of low batteries shutting down the radio meaning that once the plane lost its way it was unable to ask for assistance and ran out of fuel and crashed before land could be found.

For others the missing Douglas DC-3 is another victim of the Bermuda Triangle. Suggestions concerning the fate of flight NC16003 range from UFO abduction to magnetic waves interfering with the Douglas DC-3 compass bearings and radio transmissions.

The Mystery of the Great Isaac Lighthouse

It is a truth universally acknowledged that to be a lighthouse keeper is probably one of the more isolated tasks a man could work at. It is also true that some lighthouses are more inhospitable than others. For many the task of manning a lighthouse on a Bahamian island is infinitely preferable to manning a similar structure in the Outer Hebrides. Our next story suggests that this may not always be the case.

Becoming operational in 1859 the 152 foot tall Great Isaac Lighthouse was originally erected in the hope of keeping merchant ships carrying valuable cargo safe as they navigated through the area's shallow, dangerous reefs. The lighthouse itself stands on the small Bahamian island of Great Isaac Cay, around 20 miles north east of the Bimini Islands.

Great Isaac Cay is formed from a giant coral head which rising only a few feet out of the shallow reefs which surround it. The terrain is sharp and difficult to traverse. The area is best described as inhospitable and is only accessible by boat. Great Isaac Cay is located firmly within the Bermuda Triangle.

Local folklore tells of a ship which was wrecked on Great Isaac Cay in the nineteenth century. With the exception of one young infant all on board were killed. Local people believe that the infant's mother, referred to as the Grey Lady, can often be seen roaming the island. On a night of a full moon her anguished wails haunt the air.

For just over a hundred years, up until 1969, these barren islands sole occupants were the Great Isaac lighthouse keepers. In early August 1969 the lighthouse was being manned by two men, Ivan Majors and B. Mollings.

Like the keepers of Eilean Mor, Majors and Mollings were to fated disappearing without trace. Unlike the keepers of Eilean Mor however there seems no easy explanation for the disappearance of their brethren at Great Isaac.

Eilean Mor is a lighthouse positioned on the highest point of the Flannan Islands in the

Outer Hebrides off the west coast of Scotland. When a relief boat arrived at the island in December 1900 no trace of the three keepers could be found.

The relief keepers found enough evidence to suggest that when a storm had hit the island the men had put on their oilskins and ventured outside. For what reason we will never know but we can surmise that some misfortune befell the men and they were swept to their deaths.

Unlike the Eilean Mor keepers Mollings and Majors were patrolling an area of shallow waters, tropical weather and had the use of a radio. However just like the Flannan Islands when a relief boat arrived on Great Isaac Cay on the 4th of August 1969 no trace of the keepers could be found.

Despite an extensive search of the island and surrounding seas no trace of Ivan Majors and B. Mollings was found and the men were never heard from again.

While much speculation surrounds the disappearance of Mollings and Majors there is precious little information to firmly base any theory on. Little is known of what the two men characters or histories.

We also know little of what they were doing in the hours and days before their disappearance or the circumstances which led up to it. All we can safely say is that the lighthouse was found to be abandoned and no trace of the two keepers was ever found.

One school of thought suggests that Mollings and Majors were caught up in some form of drugs transaction. Smuggling, including drug smuggling, is not unknown in the area. Theories diverge from suggesting one or both of the men were involved in a deal and when something went wrong they were both killed to the poor keepers unwittingly stumbled upon a drugs deal and having to be silenced.

Others have suggested that the disappearance was intentional. Again these theories vary from both Mollings and Majors deliberately leaving their lives and jobs to start again somewhere else, never contacting their friends and family again, to one of the keepers killing the other (either accidentally or intentionally) and after disposing of the body running away to start again.

It has been claimed by some that a local diver, Bruce Mournier, saw two underwater UFOs in the area around the lighthouse at the time of the men's disappearance.

A more likely cause of the disappearance of Mollings and Major may be a tropical storm which passed through the area at the start of August. This caused the two keepers to be swept to their deaths like their counterparts at Eilean Mor.

The disappearance of the keepers of Great Isaac Lighthouse is unusual within the confines of the Bermuda Triangle as it happened neither at sea nor in the air. This, and a lack of documented facts, may be the reason why it is not as well-known as other events attributed to the Triangle.

After the disappearance of Mollings and Majors the lighthouse was automated removing the need for it to be continuously manned. Today while the lighthouse still operates the buildings associated with it have been left to crumble. The island of Great Isaac Cay remains uninhabited but its grounds are open to the public.

Explanations for Bermuda Triangle.

For those who argue that the Bermuda Triangle is a real phenomenon there are many possible paranormal explanations.

Some believe that the lost continent of Atlantis was the Bermuda Triangles first major victim. Others go further, believing that the Atlantians developed advanced technology which lies, still active, on the sea floor.

This technology interferes with the instrumentation on modern ships and planes causing them to malfunction and, in some cases, disappear.

Many of these beliefs are founded on an area off the coast of the island of Bimini in the Bahamas, which by some definitions lies within the parameters of the Triangle. Here lies Bimini Road a submerged rock formation which many believe to be a manmade wall or road.

The psychic Edgar Cayce once famously predicted that Atlantis would be found in this area. However scientists have evaluated these structures to be natural beach-rock formations.

Others eschew the lost continent of Atlantis preferring instead to attribute the disappearances within the Triangle to UFO activity. This idea was enhanced by Steven Spielberg's 1977 film Close Encounters of the

Third Kinds which depicted the crews of the lost Flight 19 as being victims of an alien abduction.

A third paranormal explanation which has plenty of advocates but precious little evidence is that of time slips. People argue that one or more portals open or tears in the space time continuum occur occasionally in the Bermuda Triangle. Any unfortunate boat or aircraft which happens to be in the area at the time are sucked into the portals disappearing without trace.

In a similar vein researcher Ivan Sanderson puts much of the phenomena of the Bermuda Triangle down to what he termed "vile vortices." These are places with extreme currents and temperature variations which affect electromagnetic fields. Sanderson believes that the Bermuda Triangle is one of ten such places on the globe where these vortices can be found.

Building on this theory Rob MacGregor and Bruce Gernon, in their book The Fog, argues that an "electronic fog" is responsible for many of the Bermuda Triangle's unexplained events and disappearances. On the 4th of December 1970 Gernon was flying with his father in a Bonanza A36 over the Bahamas. Approaching Bimini they encountered a strange cloud phenomena, later described as a tunnel shaped vortex.

Suddenly all of the plane's electronic and magnetic navigational instruments malfunctioned while the magnetic compass spun frantically. As they neared the end of the tunnel the men expected to see clear blue sky. Instead the sky was a dull greyish white. This color dominated the vista; they could discern no sky, ocean or even horizon.

Unnerved the men flew on. After half an hour, a time corroborated by every clock on board, they found themselves approaching Miami Beach. This flight would normally have taken seventy five minutes. MacGregor ad Gernon believes that the electronic fog encountered by Gernon and his father is also responsible for the disappearance of Flight 19 and other aircraft and ships.

Creepier still is a theory originally proposed by psychiatrist Dr. Kenneth McAll in his book Healing the Haunted. McAll suggested that the activity in the Bermuda Triangle is the consequence of a curse. When sailing in the area one peaceful night McAll heard a mournful singing.

Unable to find a source for the noise, McAll questioned others on board. They too had heard the noise but, like McAll, were at a loss to explain its origin.

Later McAll learnt that during the 18th century British sea captains attempted to defraud insurance companies by tossing African slaves they were transporting to the colonies into the ocean before claiming compensation for their loss. He believes that the area is cursed by these lost souls.

For those who prefer a less sensational explanation for the mysteries of the Bermuda Triangle there are plenty to choose from.

Some argue that many of the incidents are down to simple human error. Mistakes happen all the time and the numbers of incidents within the parameters of the Triangle are no higher than anywhere else in the world.

In cases of nervous or inexperienced sailors and pilots, knowing that they are in the infamous Bermuda Triangle, may cause them to become more heightened in their senses and lose focus on their actions. As they are expecting something to happen, small incidents which anywhere else, would be easily solvable suddenly appear to be a big problem. As the pilot or sailor overreacts mistakes are made leading to accidents and disappearances.

The more these innocuous incidents cause accidents or disappearances the more the myth of the Bermuda Triangle grows. In this sense the Bermuda Triangle may be seen as a self-fulfilling prophecy.

The Gulf Stream is a major surface current which is driven primarily by a thermohaline circulation. Originating in the Gulf of Mexico it flows through the Straits of Florida into the North Atlantic. In simple terms the Gulf Stream is a river within an ocean. Like a river it carries floating objects.

The Gulf Stream has a measured surface velocity of up to 5.6 miles per hour. While this may not seem particularly strong, for a small plane making a water landing or a boat with engine difficulties unaware that they are caught in the Gulf Stream it can be disastrous. The stricken craft can be carried miles away from its reported position making a search and rescue operation all the more difficult.

Many argue that much of the activity within the Triangle can be put down to bursts of violently destructive weather such as tropical cyclones. These are powerful storms which form typically in tropical waters and can claim hundreds of lives and cause thousands of pounds worth of damage.

Another scientific explanation for some of the more unusual disappearances in the Bermuda Triangle have recently been attributed to the presence of large fields of methane hydrates- a form of natural gas, on the continental shelves. Laboratory experiments carried out by scientists in Australis have shown that bubbles emitted by the methane hydrates can sink a scale model of a ship.

It is hypothesized that these periodic methane eruptions, sometimes referred to as "mud volcanoes" can produces regions of frothy water. Such is the effect of water density in these areas they are incapable of providing adequate buoyancy for ships.

Should a so called "mud volcano" form around a ship it would cause it to sink rapidly with little to no warning. If any of the wreckage of the unfortunate sunken ship were to resurface it would then be quickly dispersed by the Gulf Stream, thus making it seem like the ship had vanished without trace.

The United States Geological Survey describes large stores of undersea hydrates all over the world, including in the nearby Blake Ridge area of the Atlantic Ocean. While this may seem a plausible explanation for the many disappearances in the Bermuda Triangle unfortunately the United States Geological Survey doesn't believe that any significant releases of gas hydrates have occurred in the area during the past 15,000 years.

Whatever you choose to believe the Bermuda Triangle is one of the most notorious unexplained phenomenons in the world.

Printed in Great Britain
by Amazon